SO YOU WANT TO GROW A SALAD?

BY BRIDGET HEOS • ILLUSTRATED BY DANIELE FABBRI

AMICUS ILLUSTRATED • AMICUS INK

Amicus Illustrated and Amicus Ink
are imprints of Amicus
P.O. Box 1329
Mankato, MN 56002

Library of Congress Cataloging-in-Publication Data
Heos, Bridget, author.
 So you want to grow a salad? / by Bridget Heos ;
illustrated by Daniele Fabbri.
    pages cm. — (Grow your food)
 Summary: "A young girl wants to grow her own
salad, learns where the many ingredients come
from, and learns how to grow vegetables. Includes
kid-friendly salad recipe"—Provided by publisher.
 ISBN 978-1-60753-741-0 (library binding)
 ISBN 978-1-60753-908-7 (ebook)
 ISBN 978-1-68152-014-8 (paperback)
1. Salad vegetables—Juvenile literature. 2.
Vegetable gardening—Juvenile literature. 3.
Food—Juvenile literature. I. Fabbri, Daniele, 1978-
illustrator. II. Title. III. Series: Heos, Bridget. Grow
your food.
 SB324.H46 2016
 635—dc23   2014037337

Editor: Rebecca Glaser
Designer: Kathleen Petelinsek

Printed in the United States of America at
Corporate Graphics in North Mankato, Minnesota.

HC 10 9 8 7 6 5 4 3 2 1
PB 10 9 8 7 6 5 4 3 2 1

ABOUT THE AUTHOR

Bridget Heos is the author of more than 70 books for children including *Mustache Baby* and *Mustache Baby Meets His Match*. She has had a garden since fifth grade and is currently growing tomato sauce and pumpkin and cherry pie. You can find out more about her at www.authorbridgetheos.com.

ABOUT THE ILLUSTRATOR

Daniele Fabbri was born in Ravenna, Italy, in 1978. He graduated from Istituto Europeo di Design in Milan, Italy, and started his career as a cartoon animator, storyboarder, and background designer for animated series. He has worked as a freelance illustrator since 2003, collaborating with international publishers and advertising agencies.

Salads are delicious—and healthy, but have you ever wondered where they come from? The vegetables in salad grow on farms and in gardens. You could even grow a salad at home!

You can't grow a whole salad, of course. You have to grow each ingredient separately.

Let's see. For the croutons, you'll need a wheat field.

For the dressing, you'll need olive oil and vinegar. Olives for the oil grow on olive trees.

Vinegar comes from grapes, which grow on vines. Unfortunately, you can't use the whole neighborhood as your garden. How about starting small, with lettuce, cucumbers, and carrots?

You can buy seeds at a garden store. There are lots of choices. Your carrots can be orange, but also purple or yellow!

Seeds are like kids. They need food to grow. Plant food is sunlight, water, and nutrients from the soil.

You'll need to find a sunny spot for planting. Wait, don't plant yet! Remember, plants need soil, too.

You can buy soil, or make your own soil from compost.
Compost is a mixture of stuff that used to grow as plants.

Worms and other small creatures eat the compost and turn it into soil.

You can add that soil to your garden bed.

Time to plant! For the lettuce, make a line with a trowel. Then sprinkle the lettuce seeds all along the row. Cover the seeds with a little soil. Otherwise birds will eat the seeds.

Make another line—not too close to the lettuce!
Then plant the carrot seeds the exact same way.

Cucumbers can't be planted in neat little rows.
They grow on vines, which take up lots of space.

If your garden is small, put up trellises for the vines.
Now water your garden and wait. But not for long . . .

The seeds will sprout in a few days. You may have TOO many sprouts. Leave the tallest and healthiest looking plants in the ground.

Pull up any plants in between.

When will the salad be ready? Be patient. Keep watering. And be sure to pull out any weeds. Weeds take nutrients away from your plants.

It's harvest time. Pick some lettuce leaves. Pull up the carrots. Pick the cucumbers when they are 6 to 8 inches (15 to 20 cm) long. Big cucumbers look cool, but they taste bad.

Now, you can make a delicious, super-fresh salad for your family!

GARDEN SALAD

INGREDIENTS

- Lettuce
- Carrots
- Cucumbers
- Any other vegetables you like, such as tomatoes, radishes, or peppers (You can plant these, too, or buy them from a farmer's market.)
- Salad dressing of your choice

WHAT YOU DO

1. Wash any dirt off your vegetables.
2. With an adult's help, peel and slice the carrots and cucumbers.
3. Tear the lettuce.
4. In a large bowl, combine the vegetables. Add dressing, and toss (mix up) the salad.

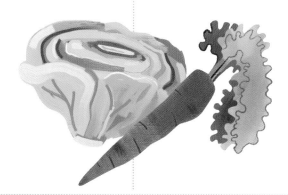

GLOSSARY

compost A mixture of dead plants that eventually becomes soil.

garden bed An area of land used to grow vegetables or other plants.

harvest To pick vegetables, fruit, or other plants that are ready to be eaten.

sprout *(noun)* a plant that has just shot up from underground. *(verb)* To push up from underground.

trellis A criss-cross wooden framework that holds up growing plants.

trowel A small shovel used for gardening.

vine A climbing plant.

READ MORE

Hengel, Katherine. **Garden to Table: A Kid's Guide to Planting, Growing, and Preparing Food**. Minneapolis: Scarletta, 2014.

Kuskowski, Alex. **Super Simple Salad Gardens: A Kid's Guide to Gardening**. Minneapolis: ABDO Publishing Co., 2015.

Lassieur, Allison. **Vegetables. Where Does Your Food Come From?** Mankato, Minn.: Amicus, 2015.

WEBSITES

KidsGardening: Helping Young Minds Grow
http://www.kidsgardening.org/
The National Gardening Association has tips on how to start a garden at home or at school.

My First Garden: A Children's Guide
http://urbanext.illinois.edu/firstgarden/
Learn about the world of fun and clever gardening with step-by-step information on how to start a garden.

Science Activities for Kids: Parts of a Plant You Can Eat
http://www.learningtreasures.com/plant_salad.htm
Learn about all the parts of a plant and build a salad with this fun activity.